Perseverance of a Withered Tree

Saleste

Perseverance of a Withered Tree

Olympia Publishers
London

www.olympiapublishers.com
OLYMPIA PAPERBACK EDITION

A CIP catalogue record for this title is
available from the British Library.

ISBN: 978-1-80439-395-6

This is a work of fiction.
Names, characters, places and incidents originate from the writer's
imagination. Any resemblance to actual persons, living or dead, is
purely coincidental.

First Published in 2023

Olympia Publishers
Tallis House
2 Tallis Street
London
EC4Y 0AB

Printed in Great Britain

Preface: Baby Steps of a Seed

Do I exist

am I blind
or was I not created to see
thus I would not perceive
such vast darkness
does darkness have texture
can one feel absence of light

am I trapped
like the cold beneath my coat
or the heat from afar
like the rocks, my feet
so desperately try to reach
is this my peak
or was I not created to seek

how do I journey above
to the land from which the water trickles

the seed presumed
that the only way out
was to grow up…

St(op)ereotyping

How do you know the fat kids love cake
did they tell you that
or did you rest in your assumption
that all fat kids overdose on sugar
because their bodies
do not fit your beauty standards

I know skinny Queens that'll eat a gallon of ice cream
I know chubby Kings that eat plants
but it's always like a fat kid loves cake
what if the fat kids love peaches

it's giving false correlation between weight and diet
and projection of ignorance onto innocent fat kids
'cause they didn't tell you they love cake
you assumed the worst
what provokes people to repeat this simile

if we stopped judging people
based on how they look
then maybe discrimination would not exist

but because we choose to stereotype
there is hate
there is oppression

the first cracker to assume
a black person was dirty and beneath them
because of their melanin
stereotyped
and built that bridge of association
between skin color and social status

the same mindset that provokes people
to assume fat kids love cake
is the same mindset
that created false judgment of character upon my people
the oblivious repetition of this principle that is used to
oppress
is the same principle that adds bricks to the bridge of
erroneous correlation

physically, we try so hard
to burn this bridge of inequality
that only exists in the mind

when will we realize
this battle is not physical
we are fighting with the wrong tools
use your heads

Nine Hours

I was sittin' at the bar with Jiminy Cricket
when breaking news came on
announcing Derek Chauvin had been convicted of murder

I have been conditioned to seeing white serial killers walk
free, I fear
I had to allow myself to take this moment in
'cause for a couple centuries there
I thought America didn't know what accountability was

they took nine hours to reach a final verdict
just to come up with the phrase unintentional murder

I found that peculiar
'cause if I aim for a muh' fucka neck
I'm intentionally tryna kill that muh' fucka

Carbonated Stars

Luminous

even on our dullest days
we shine bright

kin to the sun
the twinkle in God's eyes

He only creates us from soil
seasoned with debris
of our deceased ancestors
understand
this is why we are gold

like diamonds in a rough
we don't succumb to pressure
we use it to evolve

Heavenly bodies

that's why they're mesmerized by our curves
when we sway down the street
and the radiance of our skin
when light and dark meet

Divinity in motion

when we assemble and work jointly
forming more constellations
than the IAU can recognize
that's why we get more stares
when we float in groups

Black Queens,

do not lose energy
over glares and opinions
from bodies with no substance

most hated
most disrespected
by the vacant
because they can't steal our core
to fill their voids

light
cannot be captured
it is something that shines out from within

nonetheless
don't you gaze at the sky
and admire the stars at dusk?
So excuse the earthly for being star-struck

silly to allow them to confine your nebulae
when we were created to take up space

we are beautiful
enticing
valiant
and powerful

spiral out
unapologetically
sit with dominance
step with grace
live every day
at Queen status

America (After George Floyd. Revamped in 2021)

Where unemployment checks are more sufficient
than the income of a full-time minimum wage job
where there are millions of dollars to build sports arenas
but no funding for free education
where troops always have a place to sleep
but no space for the homeless except jail
where the life of an animal
is more valuable than that of a human
where white people are born privileged
and black people are born threats
where white women are praised for doing the bare minimum
while black women are taught to be twice as good
where the white man is praised
as the black man does all the work
where black culture is criticized
yet appropriated

where an unarmed black boy
is more dangerous than a grown white man carrying an AK
where a group of white entitled crackers can storm the
capitol
without getting shot at, tased, or arrested
but a group of black and unarmed young adults
get their heads bashed into the pavement for playing music

where black drug dealers are criminals
and sentenced to life
while white mass murderers are comforted for their alleged
mental disorders
where peaceful protesters are arrested
and school shooters roam free
where the black man cannot live peacefully

who knew
that purchasing a pack of cigarettes
would end with a knee in your neck

where murderers
I mean
police officers
are sworn in to protect us
yet instigate
and kill us
for simply existing

I pray foreigners are released
from the shackles of thinking life is better here
the grass ain't greener on this side
it's plastic
and red
splattered with blood and crooked jurisdiction

To the lizards in suits,

How long will it take for legal action to be enforced?
Do we have to wait until one of your white kids return home

bloody and bruised?
Or until a stray bullet kills one?
Will gun control laws be amended then?
Seems to me, America doesn't shift until a beloved white
person is affected
white families must sleep good at night
knowing that even if their son is armed
or engages in illegal activity
they will still return home safely
they must know that in the worst-case scenario
they'll be able to visit their son at the mental hospital

What about black families?
we are restless
we pray our sons make it home
we pray our brothers, cousins, and friends are being smart
and safe in the streets

Put your privileged ass in our shoes
imagine how it would feel
to be sitting up all night
waiting on your son to get home
'hol time
he laid out
in the street
'cause a cop thought he fit the profile of someone they've
been looking for since 77 BC
or mistook his phone for a gun
or because he chose to buy a pack of cigarettes on the wrong
day
now there's a knee in his neck

but see that type of stuff don't happen to white kids

Wearing a badge does not make you exempt from the law
police officers should be convicted of murder
tried and sentenced just like a regular citizen

Anyone who has the power
to enforce
yet continues to sit in the AC eating dog food
as if their hands are tied
are a part of the problem

Any police officer
that does not call out their colleague
is part of the problem

Every person
who still screams all lives matter
does not SEE the problem

Pee dee's
who train their pigs to shoot first then run for cover and
play victim
ARE the problem

To the current generation
unfortunately it is up to us
to FIX the problem

To live idly as our rights and loved ones are slowly being
taken from us

is unacceptable
we MUST protest
we MUST apply pressure
we MUST use our voices to conjure change and justice at
any given moment
because their time is up
we are on the move
here
marching side by side
in the streets of injustice
individual hope can only get us so far
but it is this assembly of like minds
that proves there is a common hope

For it is Faith that will move God
and our works that will move men

In the mean of the while
remember who you are
Kings and Queens do not stoop to the level of peasants
educate
state your demands
and rise above

do not fear them
they are already scared of us
if black people were not feared
we would not be suppressed
continue to be unapologetic
continue to speak your minds
continue to love the skin you are in

Our brothers and sisters did not die in vain
we speak their names in remembrance
the justice we demand now
is for them
our protection
and the peace of future generations

NO JUSTICE

NO PEACE

Is It Because I Forgot to Water After Praying?

I wanted a Japanese plum tree
but I only had apple seeds
I planted them anyway
praying for plums
manifesting plums
chile
why I go outside
and find purple bananas on the tree

Growing Grounds

through hard grass
anger issues
gas lighting
selective support
authoritative
narcissistic
uninterested
stagnant
no, because church
instigating
ignorant egocentrism
voluntary blindness
no time, but time for church
two-faced
trees
be better than me
grow taller
stand firmer
go farther than me, they say
thus, the seed sprouted into a tree

but the field lacked evolution

what are the odds
that the environment from which it spurted

had the foundation
yet lacked the stimulation it needed
to grow into what it is destined to be

yearning to latch its roots
into substantial ground
the tree shifted
leaving behind what was familiar
to embrace the new

Gazing at the Moon

I need whatever provoked the Queen of Disco
to sing for seventeen minutes straight
I want to be under the spell
that had Whitney saving pounds of love
that charm
that had Chaka staring at the ceiling
the rapture that caught Anita
catch me
intrigue me
love
connection
are ya there?
Someone who understands me
'cause they want to
not 'cause Donna made me put my finger on the trigger

I've found that
in a room full of people who love you
if none of them understand you
you will still feel lonely
in a room full of people who connect with you
if none of them love you
it's easy to feel like a burden

to feel love to feel love to feel love to feel loved

and to feel a connection
are two different things
though they tend to be felt in pairs
I seem to only get one side of the Twix
I've felt love with no connection
I've felt connection with no love
I need both bars

I look forward to the day she looks over at me and says
put on your red shoes
we're goin' dancing

until then
I'm just waiting to exhale

Feed Your Mind

you feed your stomach every day

but what are you feeding your mind?

What do your ears snack on?

Ya eyes need more than sides chile

watch what you eat.

Bad Roots

free of dying branches
hanging moss
and bad roots
the crown of the tree began to flourish

it shifted back to the field to show its growth
but was met with fear
fear of change
they tried to trim its crown
and cut off new branches
they didn't want it to have anything
that it did not leave the field with
stay they say
stop being a tree
stay here and be shrubs with us
shrubs?
You told me to grow into a tree
yes, a small tree
but why would I take instruction from a shrub
well
you have been
'cause you didn't know you were a tree
now you know too much
time to come home
why do you want me to stop being a tree

I have shade, homes, and oxygen to transmute
because we only know how to be a shrub
you must cut yourself back down into somebody we can
work with

they laughed at my buds
mocked my fruitless branches

suddenly
the growing grounds looked more like stagnant grounds
the grass appeared to be synthetic
the shrubs didn't change
they're at their peak unless they choose to change

it takes a journey away from home
to truly see your environment for what it is

dismayed
the tree shifted again
and withered into a season of darkness...

Gift

Sometimes

I conjure up every joule of power I can generate
hold my arm out like Thor
and yell

HAMMER

it never comes
instead

people stop to stare at me
and one of the employees walks over to ask if I need help
using the gym equipment

Then there are times
where I channel my inner Doctor Strange
by trying to open portals
I believe this is a much cooler and faster way to realm hop

nothing happens though
people just push past me
and the crossing guard asks if I need assistance getting
across the street

On other days
I try to find my arcana
I figure it's best I find it now
so I can be ready for the next mortal kombat
however
I haven't gotten angry enough for it to unleash
but don't tempt it

Every day though
I come to the conclusion:
maybe I already have the power
that I seek so desperately
it may not be a hammer
or come with a cape
but maybe it is a keyboard
that comes with letters
or a utensil
that comes with ink
no it doesn't create a good storyline for Marvel
but it is my little gift nonetheless
and since God gave it to me
I will appreciate it and use it

as should you
with yours

Hug Prescription

I think I figured out
why I'm not the hugging type
it's because a hug symbolizes departure
it involves acknowledging the going of separate ways
I don't know about you
but I don't like acknowledging that shit
I trained my brain not to acknowledge negativity
hugs fall under that category

hello hugs are fine
even verbal goodbyes with no skin-to-skin contact is
tolerable
because words are power
"see ya later"
that's manifestation
I'm speaking into the universe that imma see yo ass later

a goodbye hug, however
is negative manifestation
what's the purpose of us hugging
if we are going to see each other again
can we just stick to see ya
and hello hug extra-long next time?
I like those hugs better

maybe it's the feeling of departure I don't like

'cause I'm so distant
I know it's my love for isolation (extra me-time for
rebooting purposes)
that will keep us from not seeing each other for a while
it's me, not you
one hug can't make up for those days in between
so I'd rather not hug at all
than to depart with an incomplete hug

on the flip side
sometimes I find myself regretting the hug I didn't give
or the hugs I chose not to receive

like sometimes I want to hug you
but I don't
'cause I know the hug has an end

contrary to my belief
every living thing
needs a hug
and often

if lions can cuddle
as mighty as they are
and grizzlies can bear hug
as aggressive as they are
then I am too aloof

feel free to hug me
even if I appear tense
I'll reflect on it later
and appreciate your dose of love

Purpose

The door knobs on my kitchen cabinets probably think I'm
schizophrenic
they side eye each other
as I ecstatically cook for a live audience
that only exists in my head

my bed probably thinks I'm lonely
I just love it so much
I never want to leave it

my laptop probably hates me
for not getting a TV
because I don't have time to watch TV
but I always have time to watch Scandal
it probably thinks my priorities are fucked
however, it knows I'm a great multitasker
so it lets me live

my lamp is probably miserable
because it is not fulfilling its purpose
if I need light
I reach right past it
to open my blinds
so the sun can skip in my room
I use it when I want to dance though

I put the spotlight on the wall
where my TV that I'm too busy to watch would be
I am the TV
watch me
I perform for the inanimates
and for the guardian angels I can't see
they probably record me and show it to God
this is what your favorite child is doing right now
they laugh
the whole realm is entertained by my shenanigans
but I feel for my lamp

imagine being a radio
with an owner that only uses you as a stool
so much wasted potential
no wonder objects stop functioning after a while

here's a suggestion
align your life with your purpose
before you self-destruct

Fault

from wasting energy on dormant plants
to constantly out-growing
even the things it did not want to depart from
leaves began to fall

part of becoming a tree
means it had to out-grow
the same shrubs that gave it purpose

is it the fault of the tree
for expanding beyond the resources of the field
or is it the fault of the shrubs
for living idly

the tree made it enough
until it was strong enough to shift
yet it found fault in itself
for failing to nurture the fault in others
nonetheless
a fault becomes an excuse
once complacency has taken over
futile of a tree
to give life
to a dead mind

should it take fault
for choosing to out-grow
what could have been adequate
the nutrients they try to transfer now
would have been beneficial as a stem
but a lake wouldn't take from a puddle
when there are bigger rivers a-flow

perhaps
it is now the bigger tree
that growing trees are shifting to find
hence
it decided to stay grounded
and shift internally

The Drum in your Chest

I hear music

the type of beat no engineer can bite
is this the rhythm of love?
I've never heard this tune before
but I can get jiggy with it
I love any sound you make
from the drum in your chest
the clarinet in your nose
the violin behind your lips
to the castanet sound you make
in your hard bottoms with your toes
you're a walking sheet of music
come sit pretty on my piano
so I can read you and play your song

timeless times call for endless measures
and you have the notes to keep my hips swinging till the end
of time baby
but you don't need my music accompaniment
you are both the melody and the rhythm
keep stepping to the beat of your own drum love

Secret Animosity

Would a sheep
knowingly sit amongst wolves

would a lizard
deliberately cross the path of a cat

would you hop in a pool full of crocodiles

are you so blind by the good in people
that you'd shake the hand of Edward

you ask me to snatch the blades out of your back
just to leave and come back with new incisions

Is acceptance supposed to be painful?
Are friends supposed to carry a weapon with your name on
it?

You don't trust the drink
but you trust the person who made it
yet smiley hands you a paper cup and you refuse
at least he's showing you who he really is

you'd trust a disguise over the truth
yet you hate me for telling you the truth

you tell me I'm too judgmental
but I see you laughing with Brutus and Cassius
you think you're toasting with Julius
until you end up like Julius

would a sheep knowingly sit amongst wolves?
No

I'd rather stay to myself

Withered

consumers never consider
the effort put into producing fruit
they just show up to take
nor do they consider how weary you are
they assume you are strong enough
to allow them to rest on your trunk
take shelter under your crown
play around the delicate roots
and make homes in the branches
yet
during its own storms
the tree noticed
the only sign of life
was always its own

I was there for them
why is there no one here for me
so the tree deliberately
turned away from the sun
until it realized
if the oceans can't move without God
who am I to think I can shift on my own
who am I to think I have been shifting on my own
He humbled me down to a stump
I had no choice

but to turn around what was left of a trunk
and listen

you need the rain
have you forgotten you are a tree
you need the pain
growth will be uncomfortable
but your branches will not be loaded
with more than they can bear

selfish of a tree
to stand tall and abundant
yet fault others
for seeking its shade
after all
its purpose is to provide
and everybody is not meant to provide

the ultimate fault of the tree
was expecting mutuality
from those that did not share its purpose

O to the showers of defeat
hail of regret
and thunders of disappointment
the storms that this tree endured
silently watered
the new roots of tomorrow

Fire Signs

She took my heart out
and put it in the microwave
I said girl what you doin'?
she laughed and said
I'm just heatin' shit up chile

Chile Please

Chile
the city of Tampa tweeted about national police week
talkin' 'bout the city gon' shine blue
in honor of the officers (thirty-two)
who lost their lives to these so-called acts of protecting and
serving

they lost me at shine

the city ain't shone since MLK
we got a peak of the brand-new day
when the white man was found guilty
I find it astonishing that they can make the city shine out the
blue
but can't shine a light on that Emmett Till Antilynching Bill
or the For the People Act
that's been left in the dark
they been sittin' on them muh' fuckas like horse dick
I guess they gon' ride till the hooves fall off chile
they done collected all the bulbs in the world
to light shit up and honor the gangs killing my people
but when it comes to movements and bills that actually
matter
they gotta put the tip in first to see if it's worth taking the
whole thing

we still fightin' in the dark chile
f u c k police week
them pigs are gone
and very much forgotten
their deaths
are indeed in vain
they ain't protect and serve shit but their own white entitled
asses
the police department makes me sick
if it was up to me
I'd ban all crackers from gettin' a badge
Black officers only
since we seem to be the only ones
with some sense
loyalty
and character round this muh' fucka

last time I checked
you honor someone when they make a difference
when they spark a positive movement
when they induce change
when they will truly be missed
right?
now let me know
quickly
what pigs did what and to who
to receive this non-deserved honor
until a pig uses his skin color and badge
to call the department out, stand with my people, and make
something shake
burn their flowers

continue to riot at their front doors
everybody go to Wally World and get ya own Hot Sauce
so we can bust these blue lights out
and burn them blue and black flags
fuck it
burn the red white and blue flags too
whenever y'all ready
we can come together
burn the country up
and fly back to the Motherland
let's see how great America gon' be when all the Kings and
Queens leave
let America be abandoned and full of cock suckin' horse
dick ridin' peasant colonizers again

now the reason I brung up the number of officers who died
is because thirty-two ain't shit
compared to the countless innocent black lives
that were taken
still being taken
disrespected
stripped of autonomy and justice
bypassed
like water under a bridge
where is their recognition?
where is our fuckin recognition?
there is a difference between an innocent black life and a
racist pig's life

pigs are caught in 4K
murdering my people

yet somehow there's a debate
about whether or not the murderer is guilty
chile please

if somebody records me
breaking a pig's neck
unprovoked
and my face is visible
it's obvious I did it
it only takes one watch
to see I'm guilty of murder
and get thrown in the truck
there would not be much to deliberate
the evidence is there
looping

so when these muh' fuckas watch footage
of pigs killing my people
the only debate should be what jail they fenna get sent to
instead
and this is very much beyond me
they're debating on whether or not they should get to keep
their job
debating on what they think is a reasonable suspension
why don't my people get this much patience and
consideration?
my brothers have been thrown in jail and murdered for
much less

a badge does not equate to exemption from the law
and a badge shouldn't shave off layers of due time

give these pigs the whole onion

if a doctor fucks up
that's malpractice
they not coming back to work
and nobody will question their termination

but chiiiile give a cracker a badge
and they think they can get away with murder

I know this ass backwards judicial system has made y'all
think otherwise
but to express my opinion more clearly:

Dear pigs,

You quite frankly
cannot get away
with just anything
in fact
y'all are to uphold the law
lead by example
instead
y'all are breaking the law
bending the law
re-molding the law
to fit unethical standards
that means a bunch of monkeys need to be fired right?
I thought it was common sense chile
y'all may get away with shit here on earth
but eventually every last one of y'all gon' have to answer to

God
the system not gon' be able to save you then

Pigs grew steel balls
while he in office being ignorant
and leading the country into regression
he so focused on reversing Obamacare
and building walls
that he was letting pigs run around like chickens with their
heads cut off
if the POTUS himself isn't being held accountable
I don't know why I thought pigs could be
the fish rots from the head chile

now when I say fuck police week
I'm sayin' fuck police in general, too
because dirty pigs are walking free
and not being held accountable
therefore the entire police force is dirty
one band
one sound
it's still fuck y'all and the clique you claim

Black people can't even walk out the house
without gettin' shot at and harassed
shit
· we can't even walk out the bedroom
yet pigs outchea gettin' parades and doughnuts for fucking
each other in the ass

chile

puh
lease

if America don't do nothing else chile they gon' applaud
oppression and mediocrity

Morning Thanks

When I wake up
I hit me a mean ole nasty stretch
the type of stretch that makes ya back arch and toes curl
and I say ooooo thank ya God
for wakin' me up
in my right mind
thank you for lettin' me live another day

note how I said God

which means I don't wake up
to thank
please
or live for
no
damn
body

if you have a problem with me or what I'm doing
take it up with God

'cause I ain't got nothing to do with me

Pain of Perseverance

nobody talks about it
your arms
how they become limp
from pushing so hard
for so long
nobody talks about
your legs
how they stop functioning
after walking and running
through endless storms
your knees
how they crack and swell
from trying to crawl toward clear skies
nobody talks about that point you reach
when you get tired of holding yourself together
when you let your brain accept defeat
when you let your eyes droop
bones break
crown tilt
shoulders slug
and momentarily you…

give up

nobody talks about the moments they quit
they only brag about seeing it through

but the times you stop and give up
are crucial to growth
perhaps it is what God meant
when He said be still
maybe you are so busy trying to move
you forget to listen
He had to trap you in a building
full of locked doors
giving you no choice
but to be stuck
and stand still
maybe you are so busy
trying to pry open doors
that you don't even notice
the ones God is holding open for you
the doors meant for you to walk through
will not be locked
trust Him

let's talk about fear
the days you doubt yourself
the trash can full of paper balls
photos you didn't post
songs you haven't released
that job you have yet to apply for
the business you haven't started
all because you fear what the outcome will be

together
the feeling of being broken down
into a state of fear
is what makes one humble
thus

the pain of perseverance
is merely temporary discomfort
in your shift of disposition
discomfort is inevitable
when you constantly aim
higher than your arms can reach

climbing was never meant to be easy
we must acknowledge the periods of our life
where we ran short of resilience
then we can really talk

about how you gaze back at the base where you started
and see how far you've come
if you lacked talent and ability
you would not have made it this far
so you shift them feet first
you go back and dig through the trash can
for that one piece of potential
you revamp your resume for that job
you release those songs
you launch that business
and once you have taken those first steps
you get to reach higher than before
and latch on to the next stepping stone

Passion

is what got you into this storm
surely
it will bring you out

Let's Keep Talkin' 'Bout it Chile (for the discouraged)

let's talk about how if your dreams scare you
then you are probably on the right track

let's talk about how the side effects of being enslaved and
brainwashed
started the evolution of a defeated mindset amongst black
people
the side effects that catalyze fear into our goals
the absence of mental reparations
how we were never debriefed after racial laws
now we are dealing with generational curses of doubt, limits,
and fear

at young ages
America begins conditioning the brains of black Kings and
Queens
into thinking that we are forever behind and incapable

Why is your son not applying himself? Why is your daughter
discouraged? Because they grew up watching, reading, and
listening to subliminal messages that implied they don't have
the ability to be anything beyond a housemaid or an athlete.
Messages that implied black representation isn't important
enough for TV, and that we will have to almost kill ourselves

working just to enjoy life because we are not born white – I mean privileged – I mean with hand-outs – I mean, I was right the first time, white. They have been conditioned their entire life, and everyone is too far under water to notice it. Subliminal messages may not be apparent to the eye, but our brains and ears catch everything. Dig deep and pay attention. They keep our history out of curriculums because they don't want us to know who we are and what we are capable of. They only put poverty stricken areas of the Motherland in textbooks and only teach us about the underdeveloped areas to make it seem like we came from trash, or that they saved us by enslaving us. They don't want us reaching our fullest potential, because they are afraid. They are afraid of what they know we can do. We are afraid of what we THINK we cannot do. Rewire your mentality.

Pros and Cons of a Diamond

I'm sorry
if I cut you
I've been under pressure
my whole life
I was never cleaved properly
I am a little rough around the edges
but I promise I'm precious and sweet
rare and divine
durable and invincible
I've got healing powers baby
let me free ya mind
we both in the sky
the stars align
the universe sayin' shoot
you floatin' over there burnin' up
let's burn together
give 'em a reason to look
we can straggle the blue
stellar collide
fuck breaks, all gas

it takes a diamond
to cut a diamond
come smooth my edges
I've been cut by knives

so I'm not too fond
of sharp objects in my space
but I'll take my guard down for you
I'll be fond of you
I'll sit still and act right
you cut me I cut you
it could take a few billion years
but we'd increase in value over time
'cause we're naturally mined
and I believe you're naturally mine
time is on our side
let's not take it for granite
the future is now
and if you love me now
in my raw state
imagine loving me
as a polished facet

tomorrow is not promised
let's collide yesterday

God's Hair

It takes patience
to grow
and maintain locs
only the strongest survive

sure, depictions may have been found elsewhere
but it is time we lay this debate of origin to rest
and take a journey to the Motherland
where the first traces of not only locs reside
but also the origin of life
along with all things the world despises and culturally
appropriates

whether you believe the truth
or choose to be brainwashed
know that locs are the universal symbol of leadership
our ancestors grew them
because they were warriors
royalty
deeply rooted
spiritually intact

to take after Egyptians
who grew locs as a symbol of confidence
luxury

potency
adorned with elegant headdresses and jewels
or to mimic a lion's mane as the Rastafarian
in rebellion
nonconformity
and embellish with beads or cowrie
whichever way you choose to tame your hair
know that you are making a statement
and that it is beautiful nonetheless
just as a tree takes pride in its fruit
to grow locs is to take pride in your connection to the crown

so precious
so admirable
as if
molded by The Sculptor Himself
as if He intertwined
strands of Knowledge
Wisdom
and Power together
knotted with Resilience
anointed with everlasting oil
from the very tip of His tongue
archeologists are so astounded by the lustrous remains
they are too single-minded to comprehend
that the art of The Superior Loctician
never decays

Imagine being Samson
who God chose to lead
with only seven locs

meanwhile
the girls have been complaining for seven years
about the "ugly stage"
if you gon' complain
don't grow them
focus on growing internally first
locs are the hair of warriors
no way we share the same ancestors
if you whine and complain
about wanting to skip or hide
the most beautiful and enlightening years of your loc journey
because you are afraid
of being perceived as less beautiful
than warriors with longer locs
only the strongest survive

You want to skip the beginning of your loc journey
and wake up with hip-length locs?
Ah
Are you so eager to move
that you'll build a house with no foundation?
Did you go to sleep at three months old and wake up as an
established adult?
Or did you have to crawl through each day
until you were old enough to walk into your purpose
define yourself
and appreciate your growth?
Quickly, please
I have a scalp to moisturize
I love my brothers and sisters but this needs to be said
hate me now love me later but whatever you do let this sink

in
Samson did not get Dirty Delilah'd for us to complain about
starting from scratch
even with a patchy head
God restored his strength
and enabled him to liberate the Israelites

it is beneath an orchid
to let a weed get under its stem
by criticizing its petals of which it will never be able to grow
it is beneath you
as the descendant of Kings and Queens
to let opinions of others
discourage you from loving your hair in transition

Understand where I'm coming from
when I dismiss you
for expressing your disgust of this so called "ugly stage"
Who told you it was ugly?
How do you come from royalty
and still not know your worth?
And the power and beauty you naturally bestow?
What is ugly to you, is essential to me
Roots matter

Last and certainly least
I sincerely do not apologize to the white women
who thought it was okay to touch my hair
(or the ones who may make this mistake in the future)
my only regret
is not educating them after they got hit in the face

I don't want y'all transmitting any racist, negative
bare minimum, low self-esteem, trashy
entitled, or demonic energies into my strands of Power

no you cannot touch my hair
stop touching black people's hair
no you cannot touch my hair
stop touching black people's hair
no you cannot touch my hair
stop touching black people's hair

touch my locs and yo fingers might fuck around and fall off
hahaaaaaaa
I can't save you from the wrath if you mess with God's hair

For the Tired Queens

For the young black Queens
that are forced to be strong and independent
during what should be the fun and carefree years

I feel you
I am you

we brag about having our own and not needing a bitch nigga
for shit
but we would love to not have to be strong all the time
nonetheless we get shit done
good things come to those that grind
you may have days where you want to give up
you may even have days where you feel like you're not doing
enough
keep your head up
talk with authority
lead with a purpose
walk down every sidewalk or hallway like you own it
and when you feel down
look in the mirror
so you can remind yourself
what a Queen looks like

your harvest will be a reflection

of the labor of today
you may be tired now
but blessings are on the way

The Art of Pretending

Strange fruits are being delivered into the hands of
capitalism in the twenty-first century
let's pretend we didn't know
say we the people
let's pretend we're doing all we can
to form a more perfect union
by sweeping select due justice under the rugs of white
supremacy
is it me or do the amber alerts only alert amber
truckload of fresh produce on the move
take heed to insure domestic tranquility
no action required

ironic that minorities dominate the sanitation industry
when all the suit wearers and bullshit talkers do is sweep
under rugs
throwing rags and hiding their hands
what can be done when the terrorists are the ones providing
for the common defense
Oh Jerusalem
these same rugs have the dust of Black Wall Street and
Breonna Taylor underneath
they will soon ablaze
and consume the janitors working in the dark hours of the
night

to provide for their entitled and oblivious American family
deliberately blind to their father's dirty hands
eye EE; ignorant as hell
these are the janitors that are tasked with promoting the
general welfare

see
you can't spell ignorant without the root ignore
you can ignore things like being catcalled at the gas station
or nagging parents
but you cannot ignore missing children
in the same era where body organs are miraculously
becoming available
the media pretends sex and organ trafficking doesn't exist
in addition to the quiet storm of side stream news about
fruit on the move
in Florida alone
gangs of white men are being prosecuted for shopping in the
produce section too long
a few even came all the way from California to pick Florida
fruit
there are forty-eight other states in America
to secure the blessings of liberty of

pretend a little and you're a child with a cape
pretend too much and you're schizo
is there a medium
I guess that's the art of it

A Monologue from my Gold-Hoop Earrings

Listen here miss bitch
You got all these damn earrings
But you only touch 'em twice a year
Can we rest?
Damn
The studs hate us
The danglies wanna be us
Only ones that don't give a damn are the diamonds and
pearls
'Cause they know they gettin' worn to the important events
We tired
We know you feel like that bitch when you wear us out
And we love that for you
But we also gotta deal with bitches commenting
On how big we are
Gettin' caught up in weave that smell like boonk and
Hennessy and shit
We ain't gon' feel no type of way if you reach for another
pair
We promise
Just give us a bre-

With You

I like being alone

                                                               I need my space

                I get the space

                        but I ain't satisfied

        what am I missing

                        I'm coming to see you

       but I need my space,   be cool

               this time I don't get it

                  'cause you're up under me

like a stove eye   to a pot

I don't mind though

I'm satisfied

          'cause I do need my space

                              but only if

               it's the space I share
with you

'Cause Parents Be Lying

If I pluck a message from my crown
like Scarecrow in The Wiz
and recite it to a seed
or a plant in need
I have supplied
a mental currency
just as valuable
as the green
in this case
money indeed
does grow on trees

One of Those Days

I have days
where I start stripping
the moment I walk through my front door
I drop everything in my hands
and in my head

if Jason was following me
he'd see my temporal lobes on the floor
and think Freddy already got to me

I like to eat
but on these days
I float past the kitchen
press play
and snuggle into my cloud

I'm not one for hugs
but it's something about the embrace
of my silk sheets
on my chocolate skin
that makes me feel safe
so I wrap myself into a chrysalis

if Jason followed my trail of clothes
and cerebral spinal fluid anyway

he'd walk in and think I was just a pillow
then finally leave to harass his next victim

I ask myself
why I choose to ball up
in the smallest space
when I have a whole cloud
to stretch out on

then I remember
the theory I faithfully tested as a jit
the idea that hiding under covers
protects you from monsters

now
I see that the world
is the real monster

curling into my chrysalis
when I'm having one of those days
is my way
of protecting myself
from despair
and recharging
to be able to fight society back
another day

sometimes
one of those days
turns into one of those weeks
so forgive me if I get distant
when my tank is on E

Summer in Florida

All is well

you know the pool party gon' be lit
when it rains the night before
and you wake up
to fresh leaves
and a baby blanket sky

henny shots and protein for breakfast
the objective for the day
is to be naked
and free

we pregaming at the crib
in parking lot of the licka' sto'
or shit
the parking lot of the party
liquor and tree potluck at the nearest whip
be there or be square

all is well

when you are not focused on school
work
responsibilities

when the only thing on your mind
is to enjoy life
which is an objective
that has been stolen from us

because everyone
and everything
was put on this earth
for the free
to be free
to love
to multiply
yet we have to pay the man
for fruit that is free to pluck
the government
for land they do not own

so yes
all is well

when we get a chance to forget
and exist without cost

we know of tomorrow
it's in the back of our minds
when we return
to work for the man
but right now
as we oil up
and drop locations
the only goal

is making it to that party
where the burdens of life
are lifted
and the only thing to do
is congregate
and exist

and since we are in the gunshine state
the sun gon' bring that heat baby
we servin' legs for days
melanin poppin'
titties tittyin'
stomachs
whether they tight or chubby
are the fuck out
'cause we outside
not givin' a fuck
we just happy
to laugh
dance
and assemble
amongst our own people
with burnt hot dogs
hip-hop/R&B vibes
shaking ass in our thongs
grills shining
chains dangling
tattoos with the wife beater combo
rolling
driving the boat

all is well

when we live life
as God destined for us to live
He did not create us
to be miserable

there are islands
meant for us to find
mountains
meant for us to climb
bodies of water
meant for us to skinny dip in

brighter days are coming
but for now
the closest thing to it
is summer
in Florida

Daily Affirmations

I see what you consider to be your flaws
they do not define who you are
they only make you more special to me
whether you have bipolar tendencies
or a little on the impatient side
I admire you regardless
I see the way other people look at you
and hear the shit they talk about you
they just misunderstand you
their opinions do not alter the way I perceive you
they don't dictate the way I love you
nor do they make me think you are any less perfect
if they hurt your feelings
I'll cuss they ass out
just say word
as a Queen
you should never let a peasant
bring you down
I'm here to adjust your crown
a depressed flower is a sad sight
let me water your ego
I wanna see you stand tall
this is your daily affirmation
that you are that bitch
there is nothing wrong with you

it's something wrong with them
they despise you 'cause you are what they can't be:
confident and free

all of my personalities
love and understand
all of yours

you may choose to water another flower
but know you have at least one
on the other side of the garden
rooting for you

stay true

Action Speaks Louder Than Words, But…

sometimes

it is the words left unsaid

that speak the most volumes

My Job in the Revolution (A 2020 Poem)

Everybody has a job in the Revolution

some are meant to be activists and organizers
they assemble everyone together
lead marches
know the facts
spit the facts
know the ways of the government
put pressure on the judicial system
get everyone riled up
willing to get arrested
the ones we look up to
to see what the next move will be

others are meant to support the activists
and protest alongside
most of us are the supporters and protesters
we are the ones that show up
to local meetings and gatherings
we stand behind the activists
to show a united front
because there is strength in number
willing to get arrested as well
may or may not know the facts
but we here and ready to give our two cents

then you have the bougie supporters
who watch from the tent
the "I don't want people stepping on my feet
but here's some water while you march.
I don't want to get sweaty,
but swing back by the table on y'all way back
to get a Gatorade or some snacks.
And here, register to vote while you at it"
There's nothing wrong with the bougie supporters
they are appreciated nonetheless
nobody's job is more important than the next

we also have the distant supporters
the ones who will post about the events but can't attend for
whatever reason
or simply just don't want to attend and that is okay
maybe they have to work
which is okay too
because who else gon' bail the activists and protesters out
somebody gotta keep working
the distant supporters will post who, what, when, and where
they may or may not have the largest social media platform
but one thing about it
they gon' spread the word
they gon' go on live and have important conversations
sign the petitions, donate, send emails
and make calls all day while their people are outside
usually tech savvy
which we need because the Revolution will not be televised
but it does need to be documented

which brings me to the next job
the documenters
photographers, artists, videographers, writers, concept
creators
who capture both the pain and the progress of the
Revolution
keeps everyone updated
expresses the feeling and emotion of the time using their
preferred art
grabs the attention of those who missed it
so they can feel it as if they were there
to be honest
anyone with eyes that can see
ears than hear
a brain that can remember
fits in this category
it doesn't have to be tangible to be documented

I'm not afraid to admit that I don't consider myself an
activist or marcher
and it only took three protests for me to realize I don't
belong in the streets
I'm better off behind a typewriter
supporting from the comfort of my home
or the discomfort of my job
and no one can make me feel like I'm not doing enough
because I know my job in the Revolution
and if you knew yours
you wouldn't be worried about what the next person isn't
doing

Everyone has their place in the Revolution

don't attack a distant supporter for not showing up to the
riots
they're probably home signing petitions and organizing
GoFundMes
don't go bashing people for not posting relevant content
even if they have thirty million followers
they're probably busy getting tear gassed in the streets
and don't talk down on someone who chooses not to show
up at the meetings to speak
they're probably writing or painting
how do you know they didn't send questions/concerns
through an attendee?
have you considered that most people don't like large
gatherings?
everyone is not meant to speak
everyone is not meant to march

Stop criticizing writers
for only using their pens

Stop criticizing videographers
for only using their lens

Know that by belittling
the contributions of others
you are of aid
to a disunified front

We are all pieces to the puzzle
a corner piece can't get mad at a middle piece
for its inability to fit around the edge
a middle piece can get rotated and manipulated for sure
but if it's not meant to fit on the edge
it simply will not fit
read the room
we must allow people to thrive where they belong

It is not the corner piece's place
to criticize the pieces that cannot attach directly to them
instead
it needs to be understood
that when everybody does what they are supposed to do
we will all eventually fall into place
and be connected to each other
without manipulation

stay in your lane

Cold

she took my heart out the microwave
but left it out overnight
I said girl what you doin' now
she said
I should've never heated it up

Desperate

I rarely cry
'cause I trained my brain
to not process negativity
or anything that may bring me down

however
just now I looked in the mirror
and I saw a beautiful Queen
that is not in the place where she wants to be

my eyes began to pulsate
my heart began to drop
maybe I am not doing enough
but I am doing what I can

my eyes are pulsating
my heart is dropping

I am analyzing my face
and body
to figure out what exactly I am experiencing
no illness detected
okay
let me look internally
I know this ain't what I think it is

discouragement
is that you?

Never mind
don't answer that
because you have no place here
you don't have speaking privileges
I rebuke anything you try to manifest
how dare you get into my head
how dare you bring me to my knees
quickly
someone come pick me up
off my bathroom floor
before this alleged discouragement
turns into defeat

Is this what it feels like
to want something so bad?
I almost want to not want anything any more
but I am too talented
so I will continue to want

my eyes could water a garden right now
my heart is at my feet
quickly
Nina or Lauryn
come sing to me
before this alleged discouragement
turns into defeat

I should call Jiminy
but it's three a.m.
is this what discouragement feels like?

Like a tree with no leaves
covered in moss
hidden from sunlight

I feel like
in this very moment
not even a vulture
would want to plant its feet
on my branches
that wither in the wind
a dove would for sure pass me by

I have to seek comfort and assurance
from a higher power
I have no choice but to pray
Lord give me the tools

Saleste

you are

the tool

I may not have leaves right now
but I am alive
I may appear to be tilting and decaying

as I attach to new roots
but I'll be back standing soon
even as I lay on the floor
my head is still high

my branches may wither
at least they are moving
a dove may pass me by right now
but it will circle back soon

because I am...

Seasonal Friends

If birds of a feather
flock together
then maybe we grow on the wings
of two separate birds
perhaps we were just crossing paths
forgive me
for mistaking all the laughs
as signs of longevity
my fault
for always being there
and expecting the loyalty to be mutual
I take full responsibility
for ignoring the signs
when I saw a few of your leaves fall off in spring
I figured your autumn came early
when I had to keep circling back to chirp it up
I should've known we were flying in different directions
then

as I migrate to the next chapter of my life
I find that I only see you
when I turn my head to look back
I thought we would fly together year round
turns out
we just happened to cross paths
during a Florida summer

Me v Me

The battles within me
are the weapons formed against me
it's toxic, I know this
maybe I'm my own worst enemy
failure times pain
times the drive set inside me
trying to stay strong
for those looking up to me

I've been rejected by many
and pursued interests that didn't work out in my favor
but she who perseveres
will have blessings much greater
than the crumbs that she seeks
I've gotta keep reaching
for higher peaks
why settle for a cake
when the whole bakery is in arms reach

Secret Life of Trees

Does a tree mourn over fallen leaves
that once dangled from its bark

does it depress during caterpillar season
as they turn from bright green to dark

is it aware that it gets healthier
when dead leaves sway to the ground
does its heart break every time
it hears that crunching sound

does it think it failed as a tree
when it feels it has lost a child
or does the complete cycle of a leaf bring it joy
are the millions of cracks in a trunk really smiles

is it tickled by the claws of a squirrel
do woodpeckers make it laugh
is it soothed by the woo of an owl
does it feel new after rain baths

does it feel pain when we cut its branches
is it sad when it gets dug up against its will
does it miss its old field after relocation
the butterflies

the daffodils

to be a tree
that gives life
but doesn't get to live it
they seem content
in growing and producing
for those
who cut and take

do they know their purpose is to sustain life
or do they hate us for hindering them
from reaching their fullest potential

if trees could detach themselves from the ground
and walk away
would they?

Even as humans go extinct
from polluted air
damaged soil
and drought
would they come back to give life
or would they hold a grudge against us
for how they are treated now
and choose themselves
over humanity?

God lives in every tree

who else do you know is that selfless

and capable of giving life?

Would you give CPR to someone who intentionally hurt
you?
good thing trees aren't built like humans

If you knew you were cutting God's throat
every time you put a blade to a tree
would deforestation end then?

If you knew you could feel God's comfort
at any point of the day
would you sit under trees more often?

Perhaps
the secret life of a tree
is meant to be mysterious
as their sole purpose
is to remind us
that life
is not under our control

stop stressing
and live

The Golden Key: A Rant

The key to world peace is everybody minding their damn business, growing away from envy, and spreading love. Racism exists because white people don't know how to mind their business, so they stuck their nose in black culture, our carefree life, our creativity, our progression, our confidence, became envious, and hated us because they are not chosen. Hate spreads like the fumes of fresh sweet potato pie on Thanksgiving Day. The flame of hatred consumes love quicker than the flick of a light. It is easier for the simple to hate than to find a reason to love. Just as the unity of black Kings and Queens produce greatness, the product of unified hate is just as fierce. Unified hate has produced unjustified murders, Jim Crow laws, and other racist legislation that aids white supremacy. Unified hate has allowed white students to come to school with wet hair dripping entitlement all over school grounds, but bans my people from wearing their natural hair (which doesn't cause slipping hazards by the way). Illinois school district, just in, in 2021, was finally able to ban laws that restricted my people from wearing natural hair styles. Do you see how hate can even restrict one's autonomy? How it interrupted my people from just trying to enjoy life? Because now we have to put life on hold to fight for the basic autonomy that we should already have according to the constitution. If I didn't have to worry about being ten times as good, being discriminated against, or making sure my locs are "professional" enough for this job interview, I too would have the time to lounge and stick my nose in other people's business. It's the privilege for me. They have all these businesses to run and golf clubs to go be trash at but choose to meddle in my people's business. Now I'm here, unable to meditate because I have to get this out of my head before I can really seek peace for the day. Let's look at butterflies for a second. Notice how they just fly unapologetically. They even come kiss you on the cheek from time to time. Their wings are some of the most mesmerizing pieces of art my God has created. They are beautiful creatures because they spread love and mind their business. Why do you think most white people age so horribly? It's because they've hated their whole life, and it shows in their wrinkles and hunched backs. Have you ever seen a butterfly that looks old and deformed? I am not picking on white people, I am simply stating facts. This monologue would never have jumped into my mind if y'all had initially minded your damn business. I admit I used to hate white people, but it took little time for me to realize that it was draining to live with hate. I've since replaced that hate with love, and no longer allow myself to be distracted.

As much as we want to get violent and seek revenge, it is important to note that these things only add fuel to the fire. We are burning up our own peace by feeding into the ways of our oppressors. I would love to beat up every white person I walk past just for fun. I would have loved to slap the white bitch that disrespected me at brunch. Over time, I have realized that choosing peace is the only way to stop this cycle. Before they are pigs, before they are crooked congressmen, before they are racists, they are humans. It is in their blood to act this way. Their brains are fried so deep that they truly believe there is absolutely nothing wrong with how society treats black people. "Slavery was legal" my ass. The heathens are at the point of no return. The only and most powerful thing we can do is pray for them and go on about our business. Forgiveness will not come overnight, but it needs to come, in order to achieve peace. I personally have had to forgive people that I will probably never get an apology from in my lifetime. People who either don't see their flaws, too prideful to admit them, gaslight them, or all of the above. I speak from experience when I say forgiving the people who have wronged you, whether they apologize or not, is much more peaceful than carrying around hate and expecting them to admit their faults. Choose peace. Choose love.

The golden key
is not tangible. It is something you acquire through love, wisdom, and understanding. The pearl gates of world peace will not open until everyone follows suit. Do not let them distract you from acquiring these attributes. The enemy's job is to knock you off track and keep you discouraged. Remember, Peter only began to sink the moment he took his eyes off Jesus. To all of the black, beautiful, and powerful Kings and Queens: if you want to continue walking on water, stay focused, and charge through the storm.

A Flower's Tremble

If you squeeze the life out of me
and I collapse in your arms
your love will consume my last breath
I will live in your heart forever

I'd rather ascend in your arms
at the risk of love
than journey on
without your rays of light
brightening my days

for if love brings you home
it will also carry us to our next destination

Perseverance of a Withered Tree

I am sick

sore throat temples throbbing joints aching deep negro
heavy spiritual sigh sick
because I lost my food stamps

I'm sick because I am vegan
living in a country where an organic diet costs an arm and
two legs
it's cheaper to buy junk food every day
than it is to buy a month's worth of organic groceries with
nutritional value

I'm sick because I'm depressed
so I caved into the junk food
got a little too complacent
because I didn't know I was sick
I am not me
she is not her
because Saleste has willpower
she doesn't even like junk food
she is self-driven
she motivates others
even on her darkest days
but I didn't know she wasn't her

until I didn't recognize myself in the mirror
until I found myself crying one night
stuffing my face with mucus for the seventh night in a row
weakening my immune system with every bite
I have failed Dr. Sebi

I am sick because I'm not fulfilling my purpose
I allowed shrubs
disguised as trees
with the mentality of potted plants
dictate the life they think I should pursue
bad roots
produced miserable fruit
I must completely detach

I'm sick because
my asthmatic and anemic ass
was too depressed to talk myself out of running in the rain
I ran anyway
because I'm dramatic
and imagined myself in a motion picture running my
problems away
trying to run my depression away
instead
I ran right into its arms
and stayed there because, hey
at least I was getting embraced by someone
even as its hands strangled my throat every night
I let it stay because
I asked God to come down and give me a hug several times
but She never came

my friends don't know what was going on
because my misery doesn't like company
and I am the strongest person I know
perhaps I am drowning because I took dry land for granted
perhaps I put being independent above my Faith
perhaps She didn't give me hugs because I had to admit that
I needed Her

plot twist

maybe she was hugging me the entire time
I had to re-bury myself as if I was a seed again
to grow new roots
perhaps I mistook the nurturing soil around me for darkness
I was covered and protected through it all
perhaps I am too hard on myself
and forget to give God my burdens

diary of a mad black overachiever
confessions of a drunk vegan
tales of a depressed Queen
thoughts of a misunderstood Aries

I am sick because I stopped fighting
I've cradled around a rock and stopped trying to swim up
who am I
is my yearn to latch on to stability
that desperate that I chose a rock at the bottom of the ocean
who is this girl
I yearned to journey above
to the land from which the water trickles

and still found myself back in the dark deep end

am I blind
or was I not created to see?
then I remembered
the roots of a tree
they don't stay submerged under water forever

my branches may wither
but at least they show signs of life
a dove may pass me by right now
but it will circle back soon

because I am
the tree
trying to persevere
oh so desperately

my roots may be temporarily submerged
but one pro of being made in God's image
is having dominance over the earth and its components
because all things were made by words
they have no choice but to obey when you speak with
authority
I can tell the water to stop at any moment
and it will have no choice but to excrete itself from my roots
just as you can manifest your vision
one can also speak deliverance

I am sick that I allowed myself to sink this deep
and didn't think not once to use my voice

but that's what the enemy does
it makes you forget you have the power to overcome

remember who you are and what you are capable of at all
times
tomorrow is not promised
command your storm to pass
today

Epilogue: De-leaf

If you feel any offense to anything I've said, you are guilty
and need to evaluate yourself before using that energy to
hate me, come for me, or anybody exercising their freedom
of speech. I pray for you. Because if you are on your way to
check me my God will stop you in your tracks and you will
hurt yourself trying to attack me. Choose peace, always. To
the Caucasians who stand with and for my people, this does
not apply to you; carry on.

To my brothers and sisters: be great, be proud, excel, you are
limitless.

I do not regret anything I've written. I stand on everything I
said. Quote me. But most of all

let me tree.